SPORTS MVPs

A'JA WILSON

BY JAGGER YOUSSEF

Gareth Stevens PUBLISHING

Please visit our website, www.garethstevens.com. For a free color catalog of all our high-quality books, call toll free 1-800-542-2595 or fax 1-877-542-2596.

Library of Congress Cataloging-in-Publication Data

Names: Youssef, Jagger author.
Title: A'ja Wilson / Jagger Youssef.
Description: Buffalo, N.Y. : Gareth Stevens Publishing, [2024] | Series: Sports MVPs | Includes bibliographical references and index.
Identifiers: LCCN 2023008725 (print) | LCCN 2023008726 (ebook) | ISBN 9781538285817 (library binding) | ISBN 9781538285800 (paperback) | ISBN 9781538285824 (ebook)
Subjects: LCSH: Wilson, A'ja, 1996—Juvenile literature. | Women basketball players–United States–Biography–Juvenile literature. | African American women–United States–Biography–Juvenile literature.
Classification: LCC GV884.W588 Y68 2024 (print) | LCC GV884.W588 (ebook) | DDC 796.323092 [B]–dc23/eng/20230307
LC record available at https://lccn.loc.gov/2023008725
LC ebook record available at https://lccn.loc.gov/2023008726

Published in 2024 by
Gareth Stevens Publishing
2544 Clinton St,
Buffalo, NY 14224

Designer: Claire Wrazin
Editor: Therese Shea

Photo credits: Cover, p. 1 Action Plus Sports Images/Alamy Stock Photo; pp. 5, 7, 15, 17, 21 Lorie Shaull/flickr; p. 9 Janet Blackmon Morgan/Associated Press; p. 11 Zuma Press, Inc./ Alamy Stock Photo; p. 13 Tony Gutierrez/Associated Press; p. 19 REUTERS/Alamy Stock Photo.

Printed in the United States of America

CPSIA compliance information: Batch #CS24GS: For further information contact Gareth Stevens, New York, New York at 1-800-542-2595.

CONTENTS

Boldface words appear in the glossary.

Powerful Forward

A'ja Wilson is a pro basketball player in the WNBA (Women's National Basketball Association). She is a **forward** on the Las Vegas Aces. In 2022, the Aces won their first **championship**. A'ja has broken many basketball records!

AT&T

Starting Out

A'ja was born August 8, 1996, in Columbia, South Carolina. Her parents are Eva and Roscoe Wilson Jr. Roscoe played pro basketball in Europe and South America for 10 seasons. He trained A'ja when she was a young basketball player.

LAS VEGAS
22

High School

A'ja went to a school named Heathwood Hall. She was on many sports teams. She played basketball, volleyball, and soccer. She also ran track. Basketball was her favorite sport. In 2014, she led her basketball team to win the state championship.

Myrtle Beach
22
21

University of South Carolina

Many **colleges** wanted A'ja to play for their team. She went to the University of South Carolina. Her team was called the Gamecocks. A'ja was named Freshman of the Year for the SEC (Southeastern Conference). The Gamecocks made it to the NCAA **Final Four**.

SOUTH CAROLINA
22
SEC
ver of Physic l Therapy™

In her second year in college, A'ja reached 1,000 points scored. In 2017, the Gamecocks won the NCAA championship. In 2018, A'ja became the school's all-time leading scorer. She was named the Naismith College Player of the Year.

NCAA
2017 DIVISION I
NATIONAL CHAMPION
SOUTH CAROLINA
22

Welcome to the WNBA

A'ja was the first pick in the 2018 WNBA **draft**. She was chosen by the Las Vegas Aces. She became the WNBA **Rookie** of the Year. She also made the All-Star Team. In 2020, she was named WNBA Most Valuable Player (MVP).

LAS VEGAS
AT&T

Champions!

In her 2022 season with the Aces, A'ja scored 20 or more points in 20 games. She was first in the WNBA for blocked shots too. The Aces won the WNBA championship. A'ja was named WNBA MVP a second time.

LAS VEGAS
AT&T

Team USA

A'ja also plays for the U.S. national basketball team. In 2018 and 2022, the U.S. team won gold in the Basketball World Cup. A'ja also played on the U.S. Olympic team in 2021. She won gold with that team too.

TOKYO 2020

A'ja Gives Back

The A'ja Wilson Foundation helps young people with **dyslexia**. A'ja has dyslexia too. She struggled in school. She wants to connect young people with the help they need. She wants them to succeed like she did. A'ja is proud to help others!

MORE TO KNOW

A'ja tells people to say her name like "Asia, the **continent**."

A'ja is 6 feet 5 inches (196 cm) tall.

A'ja's jersey number is 22.

The University of South Carolina had a statue built to honor A'ja.

A'ja was the youngest player named WNBA MVP twice.

GLOSSARY

championship: A contest to decide an overall winner.

college: A school after high school.

continent: One of Earth's seven great landmasses.

draft: The act of picking players for a team.

dyslexia: A learning disability that makes it hard for a person to read, write, and spell.

Final Four: The last four teams in the NCAA (National Collegiate Athletic Association) basketball tournament, or series of games.

forward: A basketball position played near the basket.

rookie: A first-year player in a professional sport.